RETAINERSHIP

OF

FIRST TIMERS

’FEMI OGBONTIBA

First Published 2008 Reprinted 2010, 2012 Reprinted 2017, 2019 Reprinted 2020, 2021

ISBN 978–34355–9–0

For training on contents of this book, contact the author:

Tel: +2348038170121

P. O. Box 38197, Dugbe, G.P.O. Ibadan, Oyo State, Nigeria

CONTENTS

DEDICATION

This book is dedicated to Pastor Enoch Adejare Adeboye, the General Overseer of the Redeemed Christian Church of God, who, by the grace of God, is a divine gift to this generation.

FOOD FOR THOUGHT

You can earn a name in heaven by positively affecting lives on earth!

–Pastor E. A. Adeboye

He that is not with me is against me: and he that gathereth not with me scattered.

Luke 11:23

Ye *have not chosen me, but I have chosen you, and ordained you, that ye should* go *and bring forth fruit, and that your fruit should remain: that whatsoever ye shall ask of the Father in my name, he may give you.*

John 15:16

ACKNOWLEDGEMENTS

I acknowledge, with profound gratitude, the grace of God for the divine vision that led to the writing and publication of this book.

In addition, I deeply appreciate the following individuals for their positive impact on my ministerial work: Pastors C. O. Osho, Gbadebo Lawal, David Kuo, J. A. Lawal, Nat. Adejuwon, Tunji Olowo, and Ishola David Akintunde. May the Lord prosper your respective ministries.

Furthermore, I am grateful to Pastor Abraham Ayodele Adelegan, the General Overseer of Christ Eternal Life Mission (CELM), who challenged me to write a 'spiritual book'. He had read two of my books, The Glory of the Yoruba Race and "The Portrait of a Giant, and urged me to write for the Ministry. I appreciate his encouragement, always.

I equally appreciate the following ministers of God for their support so far for me in the Ministry: Pastors E. A. Odeyemi, J.F. Odesola, Olu Obanure, M.A. Abisona, Joseph Adeyokunnu, Ola Adejubee, Deji

Afuye, N. O. Adeseolu, Adesegun Sarumi, Paul Bamidele Mutiu, Sam Owolabi, Demola Adegbile, Gideon Majekodunmi, Remi Oyediran, Oladoyes, Ogunlajas, and Olubadewos. God bless you all.

To my wife and children, may the peace and grace of God be multiplied to you in Jesus' name.

The Lord is good.

PREFACE

There is a strong connection between John 3:16, John 14: 2-3, and Revelation. 7:9. The common denominator is God's desire to have as many people as possible in heaven. This is because Jesus had gone to prepare "many mansions" in His Father's house for those who would eventually be part of the bride at the marriage of the Lamb.

It is delightful to read the revelation received by John on the Island of Patmos. He said there was “a great multitude which no man could number of all nations and kindreds, and people, and tongues.” There is a sense in which it could be stated that born-again Christians who were initially retained as first-timers would be part of the great multitude.

In this light, retaining first-time attendees becomes particularly worrisome for church leaders and workers who aspire to reach heaven and bring along as many people as possible.

As serious as this challenge has been, this book is in harmony with the Bible in stating that the vision is achievable.

For with God nothing shall be impossible (Luke 1:37)

All shall be well in Jesus' name.

CHAPTER ONE

CLARIFICATIONS

A. Church is derived from the Greek word "Ecclesia," meaning assembly of believers. According to The Complete Christian Dictionary (1992, p. 104), "Church is the whole number of true believers and only the true believers throughout the world". Furthermore, it means "all of those people who profess to be Christians."

Three more definitions: "A denomination or fellowship of Churches," "A building made for public Christian worship," and "A local group of worshippers congregation in a particular place."

First-timers are individuals who are attending church programmes such as Bible Study, Prayer Meetings, Night Vigil, Sunday Service, Crusades, or any other activities organized by the church for the first time.

Retainership, as defined in the Longman Dictionary of Contemporary English, refers to "keeping possession of something; avoiding losing it."

Statement of the Problem: Crusades are held in various locations, attracting mammoth crowds. Churches often welcome newcomers or first-timers, as they are called; but where are the majority of them after the first day?

Some years ago, the General Overseer of the Redeemed Christian Church of God, Pastor E. A. Adeboye, expressed deep concern over this matter. Addressing ministers of God at the Redemption Camp on Saturday, 4 January 2003, Daddy G.O. Challenged ministers to retain thousands of people who throng the monthly Holy Ghost Service for Jesus.

Retaining people who respond to the altar call during any programme is a way to showcase the dividends of fruitful service to the glory of God. Pastor Adeboye was emphatic that there must be a solution to halt what he described as the "Come and Go" syndrome.

If the number of first-timers in every service is retained by workers, full-gospel churches would have expanded more than the present level. Nevertheless, it is not too late because now is the season of revival, and this is the time for positive action. The "come and go" syndrome must change to "come and stay." Every true disciple of Jesus must rise to this challenge. This book aims to convey its objective and message.

The Scenario in the Church Today At every Sunday service, it has become a common sight to see new faces stepping out to the altar when calls are made for people worshiping for the first time in that particular church to rise for recognition.

In every other service, the same thing is done with new faces emerging, but in most cases, the first-timers of the previous services are always missing. If all first-time attendees of a specific church within the last six to 12 months are present during a church service, the church may reach full capacity and need to start looking for a larger venue.

The question remains: Why do first-time visitors often not become full members despite filling out visitor forms, submitting prayer requests, and enjoying light refreshments (snacks, soft drinks) served to them? Again, this is the focus of this book as we transition to chapter two.

CHAPTER TWO

TYPES OF FIRST TIMERS

For a better understanding of the subject matter, it is necessary to analyze the types of first-timers.

The first group consists of those who have never entered a church even once in their lives. They are non-Christians. This category of first-timers includes Muslims and traditionalists. A newcomer in this category may eventually become a full member if the initial experience satisfies his soul or whets his appetite for more knowledge of Jesus, whom he heard about in the message and responded to during the altar call of the day.

The second group of first-timers consists of those whose interest was piqued by what they have heard about a specific church, and they have come to observe and confirm. Their presence in the service is just to observe the church "in action" - no more, no less. Another group of first-timers are those who are drawn to the church by music. Their presence is a function of the melodies of the songs they heard while passing by. If the music continues to play melodiously and touches them sentimentally and emotionally, they may eventually decide to join the church.

The fourth group of first-timers is those seeking solutions to their problems. They are miracle-seekers. First-timers like this are present because they have heard that God answers prayers and resolves issues in the church. First-timers in these two categories are often impatient because they seek immediate satisfaction. They want to see their ailments of several months or years disappear immediately at the laying of hands. They want the afflictions and torments of their lives caused by their perceived enemies to cease as the pastor prays for them. They want employment, husbands, wives, etc., instantly.

Furthermore, they seek substantial contracts and significant growth in their businesses following prayers. Often, this group of newcomers mistake magic for miracles! Their membership in the church is based on the miracles (answers to prayers) they receive, rather than on faith and conviction to serve

God faithfully. They want fast solutions, that is, with immediate effect.

Another group consists of individuals who attend church upon receiving invitations from friends or neighbors. Such first-timers may be members of other Christian denominations. They may be born-again Christians.

The sixth group of first-time visitors is from other towns and cities. These include members of the same denomination as their host church. In this case, denominational loyalty is the reason for their presence. They will always come back another time, especially if they plan to stay in the neighborhood during their next visit. Also, in this group are Christians of other denominations who are visiting members of the host church or someone else near the church.

Last, but not least, first-timers are those who genuinely respond to the altar call by giving their lives to Jesus. Although they may have been part of the congregation for a long time, they have not had an encounter with Jesus. This was the same situation with Cornelius (Act 10). The point of entry into a new life provided by Jesus makes the entrant a first-timer to the experience of salvation (John 3:16). With the foregoing in mind, the next task is to consider a strategic approach to retain first-time customers. Come along with us to Chapter Three.

CHAPTER THREE

WHAT SHOULD BE DONE?

The Bible says in 1 Chronicles 12:32 that the men of Issachar "had the understanding of the times, to know what Israel ought to do." In our current era, we need to have a deeper understanding of the times than even the Issachars and the Apostles did in their time when they revolutionized the world for Jesus (Acts 17:6). We must know what to do by the grace of God and the leading of the Holy Spirit. The following are some suggestions for implementation to ensure the retention of first-time church attendees by leaders and workers.

Excellent Welcome

The ushers are the first point of contact for first-time visitors. They maintain law and order during the service and guide people to their seats (Gen. 3:24; Neh. 4:22; 1 Cor. 14:40). They collect offerings during the service and assist the ministers during the ministration. Hence, retaining first-time visitors should begin with welcoming them into the church.

The efficiency of the ushers' department is being put to the test. A well-trained and efficient group of ushers should be able to recognize new faces among the congregation and provide them with a spectacular welcome, akin to rolling out the 'red carpet'. The saying, “first impression lasts longer,” aptly describes the anticipated relationship between first-timers and a church. It is highly probable that a first-time visitor to a church who receives a warm welcome will always remember such an exciting experience for a long time. Ditto for a first-timer who receives a shabby welcome; they will not forget it. This will be especially true if the first-timer is a non-Christian.

Let us consider this short but very sad story. One of the Prime Ministers of India was said to have left the church and never returned after an usher discriminated against him during the service. He went in disguise to the church after hearing that peace could be found there. Unfortunately, however, he returned disappointed. Therefore, ushers must be carefully chosen and well-trained by leaders. They are the protocol officers of the church. They should be spirit-filled, watchful, and committed.

Organization and Conduct of Service

The Bible says in 1 Corinthians 14:40;

Let all things be done decently and in order.

Some services could be indecent and disorderly. Effective organization and management of services are essential to retain first-time customers. Also, the atmosphere should be appealing. If the environment is not conducive due to poor illumination, odor, noise, broken and dusty furniture, and dirty surroundings, first-timers may not stay.

Similarly, if hymn books, pamphlets, and Bibles are not provided for visitors, and if interpretation is not offered where necessary, newcomers who do not understand the local language may be discouraged and decide not to return. Therefore, there is a need to be moderate and well-coordinated during services, especially regarding time. Where there is no time management, service becomes lengthy and tedious. For example, when quality time is spent on announcements and the collection of money

(Offering). This is not good enough and should be regulated.

Environmental Hygiene/Location

The physical problems are mainly pertaining to the environment. Workers should be mobilized to take care of the internal and external cleanliness of the church. A well-swept, dusted, polished, and arranged church adds beauty to the service. Cleanliness is also beneficial for people's hygiene. Windows should remain open for cross-ventilation, and the church auditorium should be well-illuminated during services. We should remember that cleanliness is said to be next to godliness.

In the same vein, a church located in an obscure place or noisy environment without parking space for members' cars has limited its growth capacity. For example, a first-timer refused to return to a particular church because of what happened during his first visit. He discovered that he could not concentrate while the service was on. The reason for his lack of concentration was the intense noise coming from the generators and music speakers of the business shops next to the church. Furthermore, his elegant car was parked by the roadside, and the thought of what could happen to it troubled him throughout the service. The man was lost. He never returned to the church again!

On the whole, while attention is given to the premises of the church, the internal appearance, specifically the auditorium, must also not be neglected. A well-decorated auditorium is likely to motivate first-timers to stay due to the congenial environment. A sanitation squad or department is highly recommended.

Divinely-Inspired Sermon

Another factor that can retain first-timers is a well-preached sermon by spirit-filled preachers. If other aspects of the service have been preparing the souls of the first-timers for the entrance of the Word, the sermon will facilitate the actual connection. Here, the minister, being filled with the Holy Spirit, should be able to strike a balance between feeding the first-timers with milk suitable for babes and providing his "grown-up" congregation with solid food fit for mature minds.

The sermon should be spiritually enriching. God's word (the Bible) is the food. It gives life to the human soul and spirit. Jeremiah 15:16 says:

Thy words were found, and I did eat them, and your word was unto me Joy and rejoicing of my heart: for I am called by thy name, O LORD God of hosts.

Jesus said, "The words I speak unto you are spirit, and they are life" (John 6:63). If the soul is deprived of words, it dies. By preaching the word with power, we shall surely experience God's great signs and wonders. Wherever the signs and wonders of God manifest, people will undoubtedly be drawn to the church.

In the early church, the word was preached with power. The sermon delivered by Peter on the day of Pentecost was divinely inspired. The Holy Ghost spoke through him, and his first sermon led to the conversion of three thousand souls to Jesus (Acts 2:37-41).

After the first sermon, a miracle occurred that left people filled with wonder and amazement. A man who had been lame for a long time and had lost hope of joy resorted to begging for alms at the beautiful gate, where he received the mercy of God. He was lifted up and immediately his feet and ankle. Bones received strength.

"He entered the temple, walking, and leaping and praising God" (Act 3: 1-11).

The power in the first sermon kept ravaging like wildfire, pulling down every stronghold of the devil. The second sermon was much more powerful, and five thousand souls surrendered to Jesus (Acts 4:4).

One pertinent point must be noted in the foregoing occurrences in the early church: not only were souls saved, but they were also added to the church. Added here means they were retained. They came, stayed, and never returned to darkness again. The Bible puts it this way:

Then those who gladly received his word were baptised, and on the same day, about three thousand souls were added to them. And they continued steadfastly in the apostles' doctrines, fellowship, breaking of bread, and prayers (Acts 2:41-42).

Note the words "Added" and "Continued." Acts 2, verse 47, repeated the words, "And the Lord added to the church daily those who should be saved."

Again, note the word ''Daily''. After all, services in churches and special programmes such as revivals and crusades are almost daily occurrences in Christendom.

With a definitive promise of "greater works" in John 14:12, present-day preachers of the word should surpass the ministerial exploits of the early church. It is my prayer that we shall get there soonest in Jesus' name.

Workers' Attitudes and Behavior

A formidable workforce is required. Workers are individuals who are believed to have genuine experience of salvation, sanctification, and the baptism of the Holy Spirit. They are in partnership with God and Jesus.

Workers collaborate as a team with the pastor. They must be humble, punctual, accurate, committed to accomplishing set goals, and ready to endure (II Tim. 2:3; Neh. 4:6, II Cor. 12:15).

Furthermore, workers should be friendly, able to meet, greet, and interact with people, using a warm smile and a firm handshake when necessary. They should exhibit a sense of decorum while performing their work by saying the right things, having good manners, and dressing appropriately in a biblical way, etc.

All workers are disciples and should, therefore, be disciplined individuals (John 15:8). Their relationship with Christ presupposes that workers should build a healthy relationship with first-timers. The most important duty of workers is to save and retain souls (John 15:16). Understanding how this is done would significantly impact first-timers in a positive way.

Workers must avoid segregation, caucuses, or groups in the church. For instance, some people, including workers in the church, come for business connections. If a first-timer is perceived as not wealthy or lacking business "value," he or she may be deserted. This is not right and could be very discouraging.

For first-timers to be retained, workers must show care, be extremely friendly, and do the following:

• Clap for Jesus as newcomers rise up.

• Shake their hands as they stand up.

• Clap for Jesus as they step out to the altar.

• Leaders of key departments (Men, Women, Youth, Elders) among the workers should rise up and welcome them.

• Pray earnestly in the spirit for them. The minister also prays that their expectations for the upcoming event will be fulfilled. And that they can be retained in the Church.

• Clap for Jesus as they go to the vestry for reception and counseling.

Beloved, are you a worker reading this book? If yes, you are likely to be held responsible if your attitude does not positively influence the retention of first-timers who "should be saved" (Acts 2:47). First-time believers who are saved automatically transform into believers who, for emphasis, should be "added to the Lord" (Acts 5:14).

Are you a worker of light? Hear what the Bible says about your role in retaining first-time visitors:

We then, as workers together with Him, I beseech you also that you receive not the grace of God in vain (II Cor. 6:1).

For we are His workmanship, created in Christ Jesus unto good works which God had ordained beforehand, we should walk in them (Eph. 2:10).

You will not disappoint God in Jesus' name.

Good and Quality Music

Majority of first-time listeners are likely to respond positively to music, although the way they react will depend on their background and interests. Excellent music, that is, a good selection and rendition of songs by the choir, could play a very significant role in retaining first-time attendees. Not just any song, but spirit-filled ones. Not making noise.

Choristers must have an encounter with Christ during 'singspiration'. For example, the music from David refreshed the spirit of King Saul (1 Samuel 16:23).

It is high time good choristers know that they are also significantly involved in the task of retaining first-timers. Their songs are capable of attracting the glory of God (II Chronicles 5: 13-14). No wonder Pastor Adeboye said, "It takes a good choir to bring down the presence of God." It goes without any controversy, therefore, that when the auditorium is filled with the presence of God, it is difficult for first-timers to "escape." Let good choristers with ears hear what the spirit is saying to them.

Effective Counseling

A counselor is someone who provides advice or suggestions to others to help them solve their problems. The counselors meet the first-timers after they have been recognized and called out to the altar. In fulfillment of Isaiah's prophecy, Jesus Christ ministered on earth as a wonderful counselor. He guided, instructed, rebuked, encouraged, and assisted people (Isaiah 9:6; Prov. 9:8, 15:5; Heb. 12:5-11).

Counselling, as an important aspect of the church, cannot be overemphasized in retaining first-timers (Prov. 11:14, Prov. 15:22). The way Jesus Christ counseled the Samaritan woman in John 4:7-26 led to her salvation and transformation. She was the first person to preach the gospel to the Gentiles (John 4:28-30, 39). Since He (the Lord Jesus) is our model, the church must equally do the same to retain first-time visitors.

Pastoral Chat

A brief chat and prayer after the service by the pastor is recommended, especially for non-Christian miracle seekers and first-time visitors seeking solutions.

The way the pastor attends to them should be cordially superb. He or she should be guided by the Holy Spirit and strive to be the epitome of humility.

Writing on "Are Customers Always Right?" In Open Heavens, Volume Seven (Wednesday, 27th June 2007), Pastor E. A. Adeboye warned all pastors and ministers to be careful in how they treat their "customers," whom he described as first-timers. The first-timers, he explained, are in the church to purchase some products (spiritual services). He, therefore, warned that if they are treated **shabbily like they don't matter**, such people **may never repeat their visit and become customers (converts)**.

According to Pastor Adeboye, church leaders, and by extension, workers, should not argue with first-timers or publicly embarrass them. Give them a good first impression.

Treat them like royalty. You can be sure they will become your customers.

Are you a pastor or minister reading this book? If yes, remember that the words of spiritual leaders like

Pastor Adeboye are indeed words of wisdom. Therefore, seek wisdom and understanding.

For pastors and church workers who may think that the fate of first-timers is exclusively determined by the counselors, they must realize that as people in authority, their actions and inactions will be viewed much more seriously by God. After all, it is often said that "to whom much is given, much is required."

As a man of divine understanding, Pastor E. A. Adeboye warned those who care to listen. In his words: "It is a crime to allow newborn babies delivered into our hands by God to die."

I pray that pastors will not miss their crown of glory in heaven in Jesus' name.

The Role of Prayer

A very essential tool for retaining first-timers is prayer. Since time immemorial, the power of the church has depended on prayer. "The effective fervent prayer of a righteous man avails much" (James 5:16). Prayer serves as the invisible transmission line from God (the source of power) to the church (the needy recipients).

In science, a principle states that power flows from a region of high potential to one of low potential, as long as there is a connection. Prophet Isaiah appears to be conveying the message that "He (God) gives power to the faint; and to those who have no might, He increases strength" (Isaiah 40:28-31).

In the Bible, much is said about Jesus' prayer life. He rose early in the morning to pray (Mark 1:35), went alone to pray (Luke 5:15, 16), and prayed all night (Luke 6:12) many times. Jesus was addicted to prayer. He combined prayers with fasting (Mk.). 9:29). After Jesus ascended into heaven, the disciples held a prolonged prayer meeting in the upper room. They found prayer necessary and interesting. It was a secret of power and victory. The results were the salvation of souls, healing, and the birth of the early church (Acts 1:14; 14-15, 9:32-35).

A large-scale retention of first-time believers through persistent prayers is possible, and the early church experienced this. The Bible records it thus:

And when they had prayed, the place was shaken where they were assembled.

They were all filled with the Holy Ghost, and they spoke the word of God with boldness. And the multitude of those who believed were of one heart and of one soul (Acts 4:31-37).

It is not an easy task to snatch souls from the devil that are destined for hell. The church must wrestle for them prayerfully. The Bible says, in Ephesians. 6:12.

For we wrestle not against flesh and blood but against principalities, against powers, against the rulers of darkness of this world, against the spiritual wickedness in high places.

All categories of workers (pastors, ministers, etc.) often discover that they preach effectively, accurately, and powerfully when they pray fervently before their ministries. Talks and messages are delivered with divine ease through prayer ministers. The prayerful church has the power to bind and loose, control and restrain Satan and his agents, decree and command.

During the church service, in a congregation engaged in prayer, the Holy Spirit typically prevails over Satan in the battle for the souls of first-time attendees. Consequently, unsaved individuals accept Christ after the altar call. This is the result of prayers offered by the church in alignment with God's will, particularly during workers' prayer meetings before the main Sunday service.

For those who claim to be prayer warriors in the Church, it is not yet time to be at ease in Zion (Amos 6:1). The spiritual battle for retaining first-time visitors must not be taken lightly. As a prayerful master, Jesus commanded us to pray to God to send laborers into His harvest (Matt.). 9:38). In a similar vein, Pastor E. A. Adeboye noted that "Prayer warriors are the engine in the car."

Beloved, are you a prayer warrior reading this book? Arise as a soldier of Christ. Blow the trumpet of warfare. March into the battlefield. Decree and say, "Father, retain the first-timers as labourers in your harvest." Pray in Jesus' name.

Efficient Welfare Services

The church must urgently recognize the needs of first-time visitors and attend to them appropriately. These include the following:

• Spiritual food/the word of God (John 2:15; I Peter 2:22)

• Protection (John 10:10-12)

• Material needs (food, clothing, gifts, etc.) Matt. 25:34-40)

• Encouragement (Acts 14:21-22)

• Assistance and direction (John 13:15)

• Intercession (Luke 18:1, 2 Timothy 1:3)

• Communion and fellowship (Gen. 43:27; Ex. 18:7; I Chr. 18:10).

The welfare department should be able to support individuals' material needs. As a matter of fact, they should inquire about their well-being. In the Bible, Joseph inquired about the well-being of his father to his brothers (Gen. 43:27). So, it is important to ask welfare questions from the first-timers (Neh. 2:10; Exo. 18:7; 1 Cor. 18:10).

In addition, the church must frequently reach out to first-timers through efficient welfare services if they are to be retained. This could be done by personal contact (1 Thess. 2:7-8), delegation (1 Corinthians. 4:17), correspondence (Acts 15:20), telephone calls, and text messages. Notes and letters were great instruments used by Paul, the apostle, to reach out to newcomers and new converts in the early church.

We must appreciate the need for special care of the young ones among the first-timers. The great Apostle Paul described how he and his associates treated the new believers in Thessalonica. Read 1 Thessalonians 3:1-end to find information about him.

The church must realize that first-timers will need encouragement and assistance to prevent them from returning to the world. The church must offer companionship and a listening ear for scripture in order to retain its members.

They could be given gifts such as tracts, handkerchiefs, pens, books, etc., as the case may be. After all, Acts 2:42-45 shows how brethren fellowshipped together by breaking bread and sharing their possessions based on their needs. Where there is no competent minister to head the Welfare Department, the pastor's wife should take over (Proverbs 27:23).

Lively Sunday School

Next to the first-timers' reception area is the Sunday School Department. From the Ushers' department, first-time visitors are likely to experience the teachings of the Sunday School Class, often referred to as the "bread of life." While a non-Christian first-timer who has been convicted by the Holy Spirit sits in rapt attention to listen to the teacher, the first-timer who has come for music or miracles may be bored unless the teaching is delivered in a lively and knowledgeable manner by an experienced teacher filled with the Holy Spirit.

An Efficient House Fellowship System

House Fellowship refers to a group of individuals gathering at a specified time in a church member's house. It is an avenue for brethren to praise God, pray, plan, play, love, care, share, counsel, grow together, and do things in common to the glory of God.

During the earthly ministry of Jesus, private houses were used to spread the gospel through prayer, healing, and deliverance. New converts were retained (Matt. 2:11; 8:14-16; Mark 2:1; 5:38). During the apostolic era, house fellowships played a crucial role in church growth (Acts 12:11-17; 1 Cor. 16:19). There were house fellowship centers in the homes of Cornelius (Acts 10:24), Philemon (Philemon 1:1-2), and Lydia (Acts 16:40), to mention just a few. The centers in the homes of Aquila, Priscilla, and Nymphas grew to become churches (1 Corinthians 16:19; Col. 4:15).

To the glory of God, more than two House Fellowship centers have evolved into full-scale Parishes of the

Redeemed Christian Church of God in locations where I served as a Pastor between 2000 and 2007.

The nature and operation of house fellowships make it one of the best ways to sustain the interest of first-timers and retain them in the mother church. House fellowship centers are considered as "small churches" affiliated with the main church. No first-timer will leave the center where the teachers have an excellent spirit of God in them. Due to its unique operational nature, newcomers and converts quickly become active in the House Fellowship center. Gifts, talents, and potentials of the new members are easily recognized and utilized and maximized.

It is recommended that counselors who meet first-timers after the service or program ensure that their contact information is shared with House Fellowship leaders at the nearest centers to the newcomers' residences for spiritual guidance and support. If adopted, more new members will be retained in the church.

Follow-Up

Another method for retaining first-timers is for the church as a whole to place a high premium on follow-up and visitation. Without any controversy, following up with first-time attendees is a crucial aspect that the church must seriously consider in order to retain them.

Follow-up on Biblical doctrine must be thoroughly explored by the church. This can be seen in the following scriptural references:

- It is a command of our Lord Jesus Christ (Mark 16:15-16)

- The example of Christ (Matt. 28:9-10; John 21:1-17)

- The example of Apostle Paul (Acts 14:21-22; Gal. 2:1)

- The example of God (Gen. 3:8; John 3:16).

Due to the serious nature of our subject matter, especially as it affects new converts who are also first-timers to the salvation experience, we shall elaborate and devote additional focus on follow-up in the next chapter.

Occasional Celebration of First-Timers

The Bible is very clear on how heaven feels about a person who transitions from darkness into the marvelous light of Jesus. Luke 15:7 says:

I say unto you, that likewise joy shall be in heaven over one sinner that repents.

Joy precedes celebration. It is the will of God that those who are welcomed into His kingdom be celebrated. Heaven joyfully celebrates the entry of first-timers into the experience of salvation. Given this reality, we on Earth have no choice but to do the same. After all, Jesus instructed all the faithful disciples to do the will of God here on earth. Hear Him:

Our Father who art in heaven, hallowed be thy name. Thy kingdom come, Thy will be done on earth, as it is done in heaven (Matthew 6:9-10)

Occasional recognition of first-time achievements could be held quarterly or every other month. They will be invited to stay for a special reception (a Christian gathering) immediately after the benediction, within the church premises. That is, a place specially arranged for reception.

An occasional forum of this nature allows the leadership to freely interact with first-timers. Their views should be sought on church programs and activities. Their suggestions should be noted. More importantly, heads of departments should be in attendance to promote their departments to the new members, aiming to motivate them to serve the Lord. It is my considered opinion that these occasional interactions present a golden opportunity for the church leadership to encourage first-timers joined the doctrinal class on their way to becoming workers in the cadre. If possible, there could be a group photograph taken by the church leadership with the new members to commemorate the event.

Let me add, in parenthesis, that there is nothing excessive when done in a godly manner, as long as it is aimed at recruiting soldiers into the Army of Jesus who will fight and triumph on earth, and ultimately find glory in heaven. Hallelujah.

Integrity

The Complete Christian Dictionary (1992) defines integrity as "strength and firmness of character, utter sincerity, and honesty." "A state of being undivided and completeness" (p. 355). It further clarifies that character is about "honesty."

Many church leaders and workers lack integrity in their relationships. God-given honesty is not a part of their lives and ministries. When someone says "good morning," it is advisable for the listener to look out the window to confirm that it is indeed morning.

Integrity is knowing and upholding the truth at all times. That is, asserting that what is right is right and what is wrong is wrong, regardless of circumstances.

For example, when the Babylonian king decided to raise and nourish young leaders among the Jews in captivity by appointing them a portion of his meal and wine on a daily basis, Daniel stood his ground. He refused to defile himself with the king's food. He exhibited integrity. Daniel said, "Others may eat and drink unlawfully, but I will not."

But Daniel purposed in his heart that he would not defile himself with the portion of the king's meat, nor with the wine which he drank: therefore he requested of the prince of the eunuchs that he might not defile himself (Dan. 1:18).

In another instance, when King Darius signed a decree forbidding anyone in Babylon to pray to God except his idol, Daniel demonstrated integrity.

Now when Daniel knew that the writing was signed, he went into his house; and his window being open in his chamber toward Jerusalem, he kneeled down upon his knees three times a day, and prayed, and gave thanks before his God, as he did a fore time (Dan. 6:10).

The results were tremendous. Daniel excelled far above his contemporaries. He had more understanding in all visions and dreams than anyone in all matters of wisdom and understanding in the entire Babylonian kingdom. The integrity of Daniel in Babylon must have won over several souls and retained them. This was evident in King Darius's reaction to how the living God shut the mouths of lions to prevent them from devouring Daniel in their den. Hear the testimony and directives of King Darius.

Then king Darius wrote unto all people, nations, and languages that dwell in all the earth: Peace be multiplied unto you. I make a decree, that in every dominion of my kingdom, men tremble and fear before the God of Daniel: for he is the living God, and steadfast forever, and his kingdom that which shall not be destroyed, and his dominion shall be even unto the end (Dan. 6:25-26).

Only God knows the number of Babylonians who converted from idolatry to worship the God of Daniel. Beyond worship, they must have been retained as first-timers in the service of the living God.

Another example of a man of integrity whose lifestyle has attracted and retained many newcomers is Pastor Enoch Adejare Adeboye, the General Overseer of the

Redeemed Christian Church of God. This author has heard that the grace of God, combined with the integrity of Pastor Adeboye, has helped and continues to help those who might have returned to their old ways after their initial visit to the church.

Granted that there are challenges, including temptations, facing church leaders and workers in this end-time, our God remains a God of integrity. Though integrity, as Frederick K. C. Price (2000) aptly noted, "is not always easy, but it does have a guarantee."

Integrity proves itself every time as a guarantee of success that is far more valuable than money. Honesty and humility are aspects of integrity in the life of Pastor E. A. Adeboye that are value-added characteristics worthy of emulation by church leaders and workers who are serious about the task of retaining first-timers. Those who are willing to pay the price, like Pastor Adeboye, will surely win the prize.

Spirit-Filled Drama

There is an assumption that drama is all about jesters, clowns, and forcing laughter from people. Not at all! Though drama presentations by spirit-filled Christians may not be a regular Sunday offering, they have the potential to attract and retain first-time visitors.

Given that various aspects of the service appeal to different people in the church, drama serves as a strong anchor to capture the hearts of first-timers. The renowned drama minister of international repute, Evangelist Mike Bamiloye, convincingly presented in his books "Is Drama in the Bible" (2005 edition) and "Drama: God's End-Time Weapon" (2006) the idea that drama is a powerful tool in spreading the message of God.

In the dispensation of the church today, the Holy Spirit is the one in charge of drama. Not just any drama, but those with heavenly messages capable of arresting sinners, convicting them, and retaining them in the church.

Church leaders and workers should note that a drama produced by God and directed by the Holy Spirit through vessels of honor is a valuable method for retaining first-time visitors. One or two presentations in a month should be ideal for a church that desires growth. The dramatic weapons abound. What remains is for the soldiers of Christ to take their positions, launch out, capture souls, and retain them for the Lord.

So far, some suggestions have been put forward on what could retain first-timers. The Holy Spirit is able to make additional suggestions. Meanwhile, welcome to Chapter Four, where Follow-Up receives an in-depth treatment as earlier promised.

CHAPTER FOUR

THE FOLLOW-UP FACTOR

According to The Complete Christian Dictionary by the International Bible Society (1922, page 254), to follow up means "to act further on something." It is also defined on page 255 as "to take an additional action."

For our purpose in this chapter, "something," as stated above, should be substituted with "somebody." In essence, follow-up involves taking additional action beyond the church premises, such as visiting and contacting, through all lawful means, individuals who attended the service or programme for the first time, with the aim of integrating them into the church community for Jesus.

Though there are many agents of Christian education (Sunday School, House Fellowship, etc.), we must appreciate the fact that follow-up is paramount. If people do not return to the church after their first visit, who should be taught at Sunday School? If people do not return to the House Fellowship Centres after their first visit, who will be responsible for the home?

40 leaders attended the event. We should care for people as we see them, not empty chairs.

It is true that we have been instructed to preach the gospel. However, more importantly, the instructor (Master Jesus) did not lose sight of the need to establish those to whom the message would be preached. Jesus is saying that it is not enough for a child to be taken to school and abandoned at the gate or within the premises of the school. The student has to be firmly established in a specific class (Primary, 2A, 6A, JSS1, etc.).

Master Jesus is very clear about the interwoven relationship between evangelism (soul-winning) and retaining the souls won through follow-up. It is absolutely clear that evangelism and follow-up are two sides of the same coin, and the relationship between the two is closely intertwined.

In Mark 3:14, Jesus "ordained twelve that they should be with Him." He proposed to retain them.

Furthermore, after His resurrection, the Bible says Jesus went to Jerusalem, apparently to follow up with the apostles and other brethren who were with them (Luke 24:36).

In John 14:2–3, Jesus made it clear of His determination to come again, that is, to follow up and receive the saints to Himself. This is permanent retainership. No wonder He instructed His disciples to go beyond bringing fruit (souls) but, more importantly, ensuring "that your fruit should remain" (John 15:16).

The Bible records that God has never abandoned the earth. In the early days of Adam, he visited man regularly to seek his welfare (Gen. 3:8). In the post-Adamic era, He came through Jesus (who had been with Him from the beginning) mainly to save humanity from catastrophic destruction (John 1:1, 3:16).

Another example is the Apostle Paul. He embarked on evangelical journeys to many villages, cities, and countries. Souls were saved. Believers were recruited into the Army of Jesus. Churches were planted, and House Fellowship Centres sprang up (Acts 5:42, Philemon). 2)

Yet, they were not abandoned.

Paul devoted time to follow up with those who were won unto Christ. The Bible testifies to this:

And some days later, Paul said to Barnabas, Let us go again and visit.

Our brethren are in every city where we have preached the word of the Lord, and see how they do. Act 15:36

The Hindrance to Follow-Up

The Bible records in 1 Thessalonians 2:17–18 how Paul greatly desired to see once again the first-timers who became pioneer members of the church in Thessalonica. Unfortunately, the devil played the role of an obstacle.

Hear Paul speaks:

Wherefore we would have come unto you, even I, Paul, once and again; but Satan hindered us (I Thes. 2:18).

The reason why Satan always likes to hinder Christians from following up with first-timers is to prevent the latter from going to heaven. The satanic intention is already exposed in John 10:10, which is to steal, kill, and destroy the souls of first-timers. Shall we then allow him to accomplish his destructive mission? The answer is no.

Thank God that Paul overcame a satanic hindrance. An outstanding example of his unwavering commitment to retaining first-timers is Timothy, whom he fondly referred to as his "dearly beloved son." It is instructive to note that Paul followed up with Timothy day and night until the latter was firmly established as a vessel of honour for God in the ministry (1 Tim. 4:12-16; II Tim. 1:1-15).

Paul and his coworkers in the vineyard did not give up. There were a series of follow-ups in Lystra (Acts 14:21–22) and Macedonia (Acts 16:9–10; II Cor.). 2:13), Damascus (Gal. 1:17), and several other places.

Furthermore, other leaders and workers in the church, such as John, Silas, Onesimus, and Tychicus, were actively involved in follow-up efforts aimed at retaining first-time attendees. They took time off to visit the newborn babies in the cities of Cilicia, Crete, Cyprus, Seleucia, and Pamphylia, to mention just a few (Titus 1:3-5).

The God who granted victory to the workers of the early church over Satan is the same yesterday, today, and tomorrow. He will certainly make us victorious over any form of satanic hindrance in Jesus' name.

Basic Qualities of Follow-Up Leaders

The church must train individuals to follow up with first-time visitors, as the saying goes, "everybody's job is nobody's job." These sets of people must be:

- Born Again (John 3:3, 6).
- Spirit-filled with evidence of speaking in tongues (Acts 2:1-4).
- Incurable soul-winners (Mark 16:15; John 15:16; Luke 11:23).
- Gentle and understanding (1 Thessalonians. 2:7).
- Loving and caring (I Thess. 2:8).

• Committed goal-getters (Number. 13:30; 1 Thess. 2:9).

• Knowledgeable in Counseling (Acts 8:28-29).

• Must pray for those they are following up (1 Thessalonians 1:2; 3:12).

• Must minister directly and physically to their needs (II Cor. 12:15.

• Must sacrifice to buy Christian literature, tracts, and sometimes a Bible when necessary (Matt. 13:44-46; II Cor. 12:15). These items should be freely given as gifts to those they follow up with.

• Must depend on the faithfulness of God and His grace (II Thessalonians 3:3-4; II Cor. 12:9).

Let us end this chapter by recalling and placing on record the testimony of the General Overseer of the Redeemed Christian Church of God, Pastor E. A. Adeboye. He has been a member of RCCG since July 1973, following up with the late Papa Olufemi Josiah Akindayomi, the founder of the Church. Pastor Adeboye was overwhelmed that the founder and senior pastors of the church could find time to visit him at home on the very day he and his wife attended the church for the first time. He instantly called

Mummy Folu Adeboye and expressed his intention to join and stay in the church. The lessons from this are clear:

First, no one is too important to engage in follow-up. Secondly, a seemingly ordinary visit can shape the decisions and destiny of the person or people being visited. Third, you never know what the people you followed up with yesterday and today will become tomorrow in the Lord's service.

Retaining first-time visitors presents a golden opportunity to fulfill a key aspect of the Great Commission. It enables obedient workers to train those who are kept. For further elaboration on this school of thought, please refer to chapter five.

CHAPTER FIVE

RETAINERSHIP AS DISCIPLESHIP

As Jesus Christ chose twelve apostles and discipled them for the work of the ministry (Luke 6:13), He also commanded present-day Christians, especially workers, to disciple others (John 21:15). Jesus gave a specific charge. In Matthew 28:19-20, He said:

Go ye therefore and teach all nations, baptizing them in the name of the Father, and of the Son, and of the Holy Ghost. Teaching them to observe all things whatsoever I have commanded. And lo, I am with you always, even unto the end of the world.

To make disciples presupposes that those whom God leads from darkness into His marvellous light should be taught all that Jesus has commanded. This strongly suggests that you teach people who are actually available to receive instruction. That is, those retained in the church.

After teaching the basic principles of the Bible,

Upon teaching the doctrines to them, they are required to undergo baptism by immersion. Thereafter, they go through training as workers and subsequently become full workers, resulting in more disciples of Christ who can carry out various assignments in the ministry. The foregoing was the pattern of what was observed in the early church. Acts 2:41–42 amplifies this point.

Then those who gladly received his word were baptised, and on the same day, about three thousand souls were added to them. And they continued steadfastly in the apostles' doctrines, fellowship, breaking of bread, and prayers.

The words "and they continued" should be seriously noted. That is, the first-timers continued in the church. Put differently, the retention and subsequent nurturing of first-timers in matters of faith should bring joy to church workers. Why? It is one of the major ways of fulfilling the Great Commission. That is, "teaching them to observe all things whatsoever I have commanded."

It goes without saying, therefore, that whatever work one does to fulfill the Master's mandate will be richly rewarded. Rev. 22:12 puts it better:

And behold, I come quickly; and my reward is with me to give every man according to his work.

A true disciple of Jesus (a worker in the vineyard) would desire to make disciples of others for the King's business. He knows that by doing so, he is involved in good works that yield abundant fruit and glorify God. This is how the Bible explains it:

Herein is my Father glorified, that you bear much fruit; so shall you be my disciples (John 15:8).

Are you willing to obey Master Jesus, especially by retaining the first-timers for discipleship? If yes, I rejoice with you for your decision. Be determined to accomplish it. Congratulations in advance, because God will back you up.

Beloved, you will be rewarded in due season. Verily, verily, I say unto you, the fruit of the land shall be yours, and you will eat it as you retain first-timers in Jesus' name (Isaiah 1:19). Say a big Amen.

Thank you for patiently reading through the first five chapters of this book. The next and last chapters are peculiar for obvious reasons. Approach this text with caution as you finalise and carry out specific assignments in the king's business within your church.

CHAPTER SIX

CAUTION, CONCLUSION, AND ASSIGNMENTS

Though God, the Creator of heaven and earth, saw that everything He had made was very good (Gen. 1:31), He also noted strongly that "it is not good for man to be alone." "(Gen. 2:18a)." In the same vein, it is not good to conclude this all-important subject matter without reference to the sons and daughters of perdition. Perdition, according to The Complete Christian Dictionary (1992, p. 500), is defined as "eternal damnation."

No matter what arrangement a church puts in place, sons and daughters of perdition will be lost. Our Lord and Saviour, Jesus Christ, already foretold this in advance. He said:

When I was with them in the world, I keep them in thy name: those that thou gavest me I have kept and none of them is lost, but the son of perdition that the scripture might be fulfilled (John 17:12).

Some individuals may attend church for the first time, and some may even join the workers' cadre, but the truth is that God did not plant them.

They may come to the church as agents of darkness to work for their master, Satan. They are a mixed multitude (Exod. 12:38). They are deceivers and never angels of light, but of the devil (II Cor. 11:14). The fact that we are all in church does not mean we are all for God. "No, not at all" (Job 2:1).

A man of God shared with me how God used his opening prayer to impact a first-timer who had entered the church with intentions to carry out the work of the thief (John 10:10a). When the fire from the minister's opening prayer was too intense for the first-timer to handle, she ran out of the church, and her wrap fell off her body. She never returned again. She had earlier confessed to someone in the church that she had successfully carried out satanic missions in two different churches. She entered the third church as a "first-timer" with the same devilish intention. However, before she could commit any evil deeds, the superior fire of God expelled the daughter of perdition. Glory be to God.

While we are not ruling out the possibility of God's mercy through deliverance for agents of darkness, as was the case with Mary Magdalene (Luke 8:2–3; Matt. 28:9), there will always be some stubborn individuals like Jezebel (1 Kings 16:31, 21:23-25, II Kings. 9:10, 30-37), who are destined for perdition. If such Jezebels come in as first-timers into a church where there is divine fire, they cannot be retained, no matter how hard the follow-up leaders may try. Since they are plants not planted by God, the logical outcome is already predetermined: they shall be uprooted.

This is what Jesus, the owner of the church, said: *Every plant, which my heavenly Father has not planted, shall be rooted up* (Matthew 15:13).

Conclusion

A. Matthew 25:14–23 emphasises the importance of being profitable servants shall receive a "well done" from Master Jesus. It is dangerous to be unprofitable (Matt. 25:24–30; II Cor. 6:1).

B. According to John 15:14–16, only by obeying Jesus would make us His friends. They shall ask and receive from God in His name. Ensure that you are a friend of Jesus.

C. Rev. 22:12 emphasises that Jesus will surely come back again to reward those who work (for example, the stewardship of new believers in the church). Be diligent to receive eternal rewards.

D. I Cor. 3:6 says only God gives increase. So, learn how to praise God for every first-time visitor retained in the church. This will lead to further growth of the church by Jesus through an additional increase in the number of first-time visitors who will stay. After all, Jesus said in Matthew 16:18, “I will build my church.” Therefore, give glory to the One who owns and can build the church. (Romans 16:16b).

Assignments

Dearly beloved, if you have found this manual helpful, please feel free to recommend it to someone else. By doing so, you are also contributing to the expansion of the King's kingdom.

More importantly, prayerfully select the methods suitable for following up with at least three members of the congregation of your church every month. Remember that three represents the Trinity. As you follow up with the members for retention in your church, may the God of heaven and earth perfect everything concerning you and reward your labour of love in Jesus' name (Psalm 138:8; I Cor. 15:58).

Beloved, remember the words of our Lord and Saviour, Jesus Christ, in John 13:17. He is saying directly to you, "If ye know these things, happy are ye if ye do them." You will be happy in life as you obey Jesus in Jesus' name.

Finally, brethren, whatsoever things are true, whatsoever things are honest, whatsoever things are just, whatsoever things are pure, whatsoever things are lovely, whatever things are of good report; if there be any virtue, and if there be any praise, think on these things (Phil. 4:8).

CHAPTER SEVEN

PRAYERS FOR RETAINERS

In line with the tradition of the Bible, which emphasises the blessings of God for anyone who obeys Him (Deut.), when as many workers and church leaders as possible diligently work for the retention of first-time visitors (Deuteronomy 28:1–13), they will receive all these blessings.

1. Daily, God will give you the miracle of sleeping and waking up.

2. Your sun shall not set at midday.

3. God will contend with whoever and whatever contends with you.

4. In an incomparable way, God will generously reward your labour in His vineyard.

5. Every evil waiting to harm you shall not materialise.

6. Whatever causes you anxiety and restlessness will eventually turn into testimonies for you.

7. The Great Provider shall regularly supply all your needs.

8. God will fulfill His promises for you in your lifetime.

9. You will be too hot for the devil and his agents to handle.

10. God will enlarge your coast.

11. You will reach your goal(s) in life.

12. You will finish well and strong

13. When those whom you have chosen for God are marching in on the last day, you will not be cast away.

14. You will not miss your crown.

All shall be well in Jesus' name.

APPENDIX

Aggressive Follow-up

A. God followed up the world **(Gen. 3:8; John 3:16)**

B. Jesus did and will still do **(Luke 24:13-51; Acts 1:11).**

C. Holy Spirit did **(John 14:26; Acts 13:2).**

D. The Apostle did **(Acts 15:36; Gal. 1:17).**

2. Herb Miller, a gospel minister and church planner, says:

A. 85% of first-time visitors return if they are visited within 36 hours of their initial visit.

B. 60% of first-time visitors return if they are visited within 72 hours of their initial visit.

C. 15% of newcomers return if they visit within seven days of their arrival.

D. Retention of first-time clients is highest when you follow up with them within 48 hours.

E. Your church will not grow if newcomers do not return. For your church to grow, newcomers must connect with people in your congregation.

Note: Daddy E. A. Adeboye says: "One of the ways to shine is through soul-winning." This is the primary mandate of believers. To shine, we should make soul-winning a continuous practice until Jesus comes back in power and glory (Acts 1:6–8; 2 Timothy 4:5). Souls that are won must be prayed for regularly and followed up with to avoid loss (John 15:16). It is your time to shine.

Ref: Open Heavens, June 15, 2014.

Note: multi-dimensional follow-up system across ten contact points.

Men, women, youth, elders, counsellors, Sunday School, House Fellowship, Prayer, PIC and the entire workforce.

ADDITIONAL IDEAS

•Assimilation/Co-option of First-Timers into Family System

•Operation Total Bombardment.

Note: Further details on request.

Other Books by the Author

1. NYSC at 15
2. Nigeria: The Awolowo Factor
3. The Glory of the Yoruba Race
4. The Portrait of a Giant
5. Sustainable Church Growth in a Competitive Era
6. Sustaining the Evangelical Landmarks of Pastor E. A. Adeboye for Church Growth
7. 16 Strategies for Growing the Church
8. All-Round Fulfillment: Yes, You Can
9. Commanded to Succeed.
10. I Will Fulfill Destiny
11. God Is In Need

www.ingramcontent.com/pod-product-compliance
Lightning Source LLC
LaVergne TN
LVHW050341160826
845677LV00014B/3722

* 9 7 8 9 7 8 3 4 3 5 5 9 9 *